Main

ALL AROUND THE WORLD
SOUTH AFRICA

by Kristine Spanier

pogo

Ideas for Parents and Teachers

Pogo Books let children practice reading informational text while introducing them to nonfiction features such as headings, labels, sidebars, maps, and diagrams, as well as a table of contents, glossary, and index.

Carefully leveled text with a strong photo match offers early fluent readers the support they need to succeed.

Before Reading

- "Walk" through the book and point out the various nonfiction features. Ask the student what purpose each feature serves.
- Look at the glossary together. Read and discuss the words.

Read the Book

- Have the child read the book independently.
- Invite him or her to list questions that arise from reading.

After Reading

- Discuss the child's questions. Talk about how he or she might find answers to those questions.
- Prompt the child to think more. Ask: Did you know about Nelson Mandela before reading this book? What more would you like to learn about him?

Pogo Books are published by Jump!
5357 Penn Avenue South
Minneapolis, MN 55419
www.jumplibrary.com

Library of Congress Cataloging-in-Publication Data

Names: Spanier, Kristine, author.
Title: South Africa / by Kristine Spanier.
Description: Minneapolis, MN: Jump!, Inc., 2020.
Series: All around the world | "Pogo Books are published by Jump!" | Includes bibliographical references and index.
Identifiers: LCCN 2018046646 (print)
LCCN 2018048337 (ebook)
ISBN 9781641286589 (ebook)
ISBN 9781641286565 (hardcover : alk. paper)
ISBN 9781641286572 (pbk.)
Subjects: LCSH: South Africa—Juvenile literature.
Classification: LCC DT1719 (ebook)
LCC DT1719 .S698 2020 (print) | DDC 968—dc23
LC record available at https://lccn.loc.gov/2018046646

Editor: Susanne Bushman
Designer: Leah Sanders

Photo Credits: PictureScapes/Shutterstock, cover, 6-7b; GoodMood Photo/Shutterstock, 1; Pixfiction/Shutterstock, 3; kavram/Shutterstock, 4; Andre Coetzer/Shutterstock, 5; Siegfried Schnepf/iStock, 6t; by wildestanimal/Getty, 6b; Pascale Gueret/Shutterstock, 6-7t; Mathias Sunke/Shutterstock, 8-9; Mauritius/SuperStock, 10; Suretha Rous/Alamy, 11; Alexander Joe/Getty, 12-13; Sproetneik/iStock, 14; BFG Images/Getty, 15; Ariadne Van Zandbergen/Alamy, 16-17; Gallo Images/SuperStock, 18-19; Newspix/Getty, 20-21; Anton_Ivanov/Shutterstock, 23.

Printed in the United States of America at Corporate Graphics in North Mankato, Minnesota.

TABLE OF CONTENTS

CHAPTER 1
Welcome to South Africa! 4

CHAPTER 2
South Africa's History 10

CHAPTER 3
Life in South Africa 14

QUICK FACTS & TOOLS
At a Glance 22
Glossary 23
Index 24
To Learn More 24

CHAPTER 1

WELCOME TO SOUTH AFRICA!

Ride in a kombi. Taste potjiekos. Spot African penguins on Boulders Beach. Welcome to South Africa!

Part of the Kalahari Desert is here. Herds of wildebeests live here. What else? Hyenas. Baboons. Giraffes.

beach

swamp

coral reef

Biedouw Valley

This country has many **ecosystems**. Sandy beaches. Lakes. Swamps. Coral reefs. iSimangaliso Wetland Park is home to all of these. More than 6,500 kinds of plants and animals live here. Elephants. Hippos. Lions. Zebras.

Many flowering plants grow in South Africa. How many? More than 20,000 types. Many bloom in Biedouw Valley after spring rains.

DID YOU KNOW?

South Africa completely surrounds the country of Lesotho. It sits on a high **plateau**.

Cape Town is one of South Africa's **capitals**. It is at the base of Table Mountain. The city is along the coast. A **harbor** is here. Some people live on boats!

South Africa has three capitals. Cape Town is where lawmakers work. Pretoria is where the **president** works. The highest courts are in Bloemfontein.

Table
Mountain

CHAPTER 2

SOUTH AFRICA'S HISTORY

South Africa has a **parliament**. It has two houses. The National Council of Provinces is one. Local lawmakers choose the members. The people elect the National Assembly. They choose the president.

Houses of Parliament

WHITE PERSONS ONLY

THIS BEACH & THE AMENITIES THEREOF
HAVE BEEN RESERVED FOR WHITE
PERSONS ONLY

BY ORDER
PROVINCIAL SECRETARY

NET BLANKES

It wasn't always this way. South Africa describes the **majority** of the people here as black. Whites came to the area in 1652. In 1913, they began making laws that said blacks couldn't do things. Like what? Own land. Live in certain areas. Vote for leaders. Have certain jobs. This was called **apartheid**.

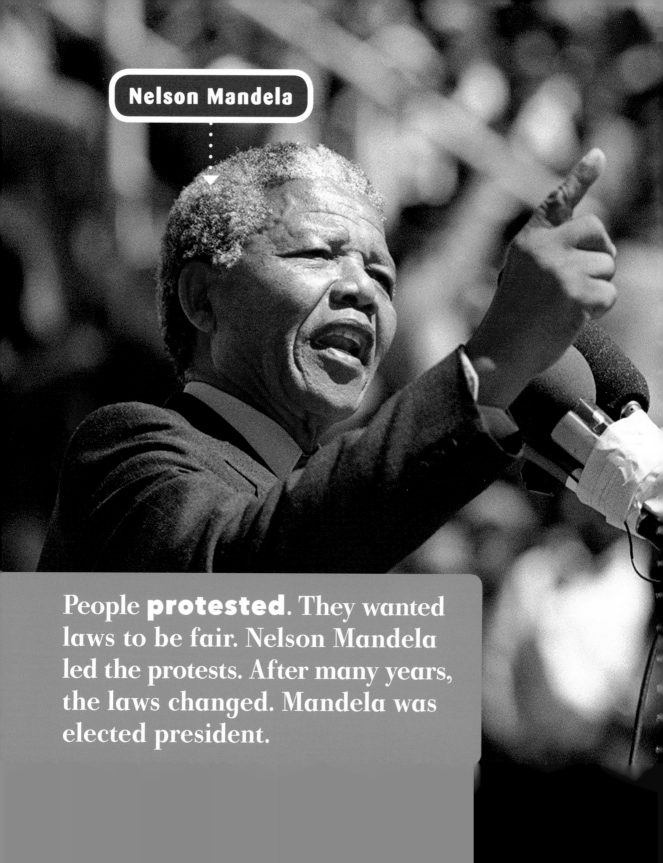

Nelson Mandela

People **protested**. They wanted laws to be fair. Nelson Mandela led the protests. After many years, the laws changed. Mandela was elected president.

TAKE A LOOK!

South Africa struggled with apartheid for more than 75 years.

1913
A law passes that limits where blacks can own property.

1994
Mandela is elected president by the people of South Africa.

1948
Apartheid becomes legal.

1990-1991
Apartheid ends. Mandela is freed.

1960s
Mandela leads protests. He goes to prison.

CHAPTER 3

LIFE IN SOUTH AFRICA

Cornmeal porridge is a filling breakfast. Spiced sausage is good for dinner. At festivals, people enjoy making potjiekos. This is a meat and vegetable stew. It is cooked over an outdoor fire.

potjiekos ·····▶

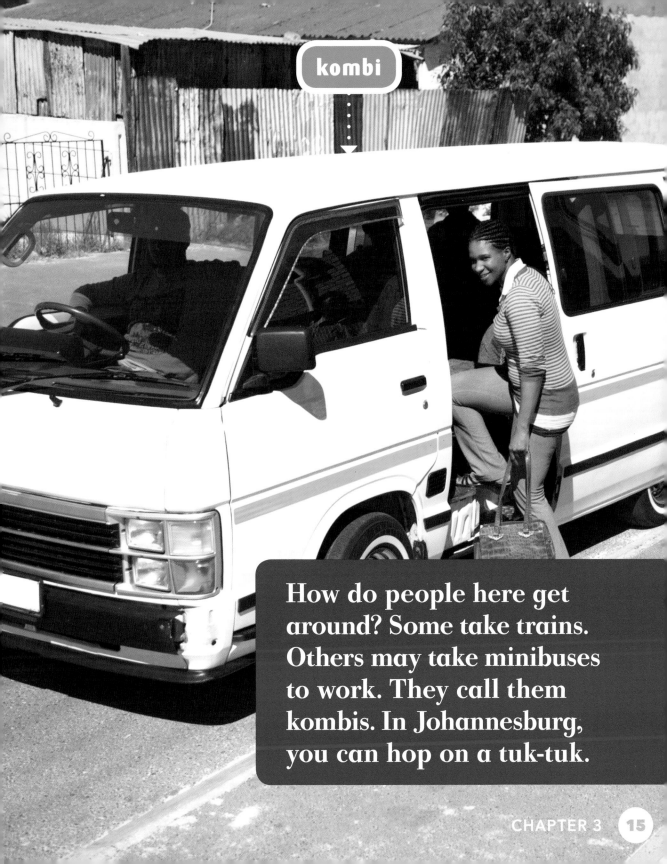

kombi

How do people here get around? Some take trains. Others may take minibuses to work. They call them kombis. In Johannesburg, you can hop on a tuk-tuk.

The Nama people still live in a **traditional** way. They raise animals. They move across the land. They bring their houses with them.

WHAT DO YOU THINK?

The Bantu people use the word "ubuntu." This means that people should put kindness above all else. How do you show ubuntu in your life?

Most children start school when they are seven. After three years, students begin learning another language. The final years are spent preparing for jobs. Some go on to college.

WHAT DO YOU THINK?

In **rural** areas, it can be hard to get to school. Why? Students have to travel far. Is it easy or hard for you to get to school? How far do you travel?

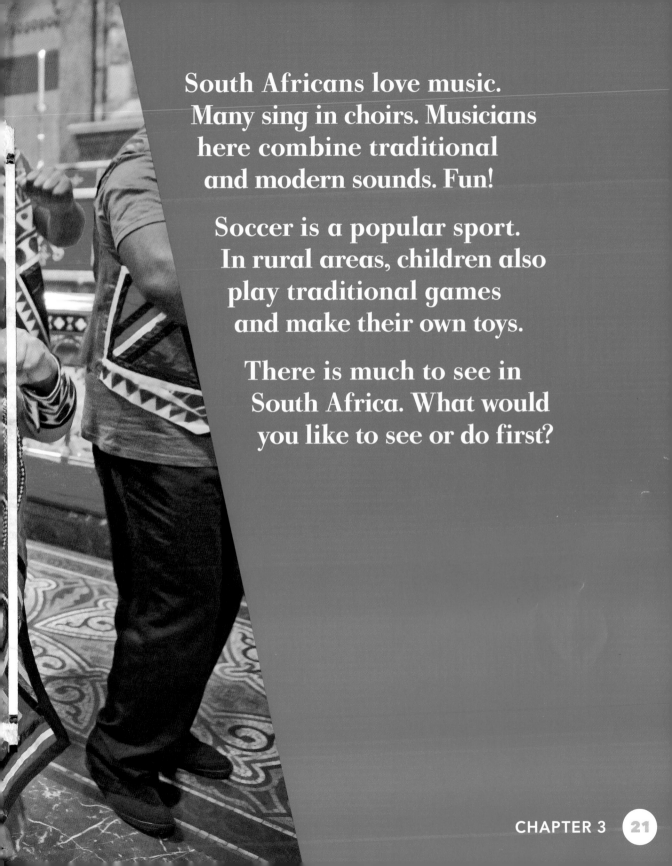

South Africans love music.
Many sing in choirs. Musicians
here combine traditional
and modern sounds. Fun!

Soccer is a popular sport.
In rural areas, children also
play traditional games
and make their own toys.

There is much to see in
South Africa. What would
you like to see or do first?

QUICK FACTS & TOOLS

SOUTH AFRICA

Location: southern Africa

Size: 470,693 square miles (1,219,090 square kilometers)

Population: 55,380,210 (July 2018 estimate)

Capitals: Cape Town, Pretoria, Bloemfontein

Type of Government: parliamentary republic

Languages: 11 official languages, including Zulu, Xhosa, Afrikaans, and English

Exports: gold, diamonds, platinum

Currency: rand

apartheid: A set of laws in South Africa that discriminated against blacks for more than 75 years.

capitals: Cities where government leaders meet.

ecosystems: Areas that include all the living and nonliving things within it.

harbor: An area of calm water near land where ships can dock or put down anchors, often to unload cargo.

majority: More than half of the people in a group.

parliament: A group of people elected to make laws.

plateau: An area of level ground that is higher than the surrounding area.

president: The leader of a country.

protested: Demonstrated against something.

rural: Related to the country and country life.

traditional: Having to do with the customs, beliefs, or activities that are handed down from one generation to the next.

South Africa's currency

INDEX

apartheid 11, 13

Bantu people 17

Biedouw Valley 7

Bloemfontein 8

Boulders Beach 4

Cape Town 8

capitals 8

ecosystems 7

games 21

iSimangaliso Wetland Park 7

Johannesburg 15

Kalahari Desert 5

kombi 4, 15

Lesotho 7

Mandela, Nelson 12, 13

music 21

Nama people 17

parliament 10

plants 7

potjiekos 4, 14

president 8, 10, 12, 13

Pretoria 8

protested 12, 13

school 18

TO LEARN MORE

Finding more information is as easy as 1, 2, 3.

1. Go to www.factsurfer.com
2. Enter "SouthAfrica" into the search box.
3. Click the "Surf" button to see a list of websites.

FACT SURFER